Inside a
VICTORIAN HOUSE

The National Trust

Illustrated by Dai Owen

The House and its Surroundings

This house has been created from different parts of
Victorian houses owned by the National Trust to
show you what life was like for a rich family and their
servants one hundred years ago.

Many Victorians made their fortunes from industries such as cotton,
wool and iron, and the new railways that were spreading across the
country. These factory owners and engineers wanted a grand house
and estate to show off their new wealth.

THE BUSINESS OF THE
ESTATE WAS ARRANGED
IN THE ESTATE OFFICE

DOVES WERE KEPT
IN A DOVECOTE
FOR DECORATION,
NOT FOR MEAT

THE COACH HOUSE
WAS PART OF
THE STABLE BLOCK

DAIRY

LAUNDRY

CONSERVA

THERE WAS PLENTY
OF ROOM IN FRONT
OF THE HOUSE FOR
THE CARRIAGES
TO TURN

HOME FARM

APPLES, PEARS AND PLUMS WERE GROWN IN THE ORCHARD

SHEEP GRAZED IN THE ESTATE FIELDS. MUTTON WAS A POPULAR MEAT IN VICTORIAN TIMES

RIVER

WALLED KITCHEN GARDEN

ORNAMENTAL LAKE

DEER BARN

THE PARK

THE FORMAL GARDENS

DEER WERE KEPT AS AN ATTRACTIVE ADDITION TO THE PARK, NOT TO BE HUNTED

THE LODGE STOOD AT THE ENTRANCE TO THE DRIVE

The estate provided most of the things the family needed. Vegetables and fruit came from the kitchen garden; fish from the rivers; meat, milk and eggs from the home farm; and timber from the estate woods.

The Entrance

Visitors would arrive at the house in a horse-drawn carriage. The butler would be at the front door to welcome them, with more staff ready to carry luggage into the house. The carriage would then be taken round to the stables, where the horses could be fed and rested.

THE MAIN ENTRANCE TO THE HOUSE WAS ALWAYS QUITE GRAND TO IMPRESS VISITORS

BUTLER

HORSES WORE BLINKERS TO MAKE SURE THEY ONLY LOOKED AT THE ROAD AHEAD

THE HOOD ONLY COVERED THE BACK SEATS

THE STABLE BOY WAS AT HAND TO LOOK AFTER THE TIRED HORSES

THE COACHMAN WORE HIS LIVERY OR UNIFORM

AN ELEGANT TYPE OF CARRIAGE WAS SUITABLE FOR ENJOYING THE COUNTRYSIDE. IT WAS BUILT NEAR THE GROUND TO MAKE IT EASIER FOR WOMEN IN LARGE DRESSES TO CLIMB IN AND OUT

The Servants

A large house could have had as many as fifty servants: the butler was in charge of all the male servants; the housekeeper supervised the housemaids, and the cook organised the kitchenmaids.

Between them, the staff had all the different skills needed to make the household run smoothly.

GROOM COACHMAN HOUSEMAIDS LADY'S MAID SCULLERYMAIDS GARDENERS

STABLEBOY

FOOTMEN BUTLER HOUSEKEEPER COOK KITCHENMAIDS GAMEKEEPER

THE SERVANTS WORKED VERY HARD FROM EARLY IN THE MORNING UNTIL LATE AT NIGHT, AND ONLY HAD ONE DAY OFF A MONTH

THE FIRST PHOTOGRAPHS WERE TAKEN IN EARLY VICTORIAN TIMES, AND MANY FAMILIES WERE KEEN ON THIS NEW INVENTION. A FEW HOUSEOWNERS EVEN TOOK PHOTOS OF THEIR SERVANTS

The Drawing Room

On arrival, guests would be shown into the Drawing Room. In Victorian times it was fashionable to fill rooms with lots of furniture. Pictures, photographs and ornaments added to the clutter. The walls and floors were decorated with expensive patterned wallpapers and carpets.

THE MANTLEPIECE WAS USUALLY VERY IMPRESSIVE, WITH A FINE CLOCK AND MIRRORS ABOVE

THE WALLPAPER PATTERNS WERE OFTEN IN DARK COLOURS

A FIRESCREEN KEPT THE HEAT FROM PEOPLE'S FACES

TABLES WERE USUALLY COVERED WITH A CLOTH – VICTORIANS THOUGHT IT WAS IMPROPER TO SHOW THE LEGS

The Victorians enjoyed games and musical entertainment. In the Drawing Room the family and guests often played cards. Young ladies were expected to learn the piano and in some houses there was a special music room.

Children were allowed into the Drawing Room if they sat quietly and only spoke when they were spoken to. Ladies would pass the time by reading or sewing.

The Library

This was a gentleman's room. Important collections of books, prints and atlases would be displayed on the shelves. The owner of the house might have written his letters in here: everything he needed was on the desk. There was often a secret door in the Library, disguised as a bookcase, for servants to use. The Victorians felt that servants should be kept out of sight as much as possible.

STAINED GLASS WAS OFTEN USED IN THE TOP LIGHTS OF THE WINDOW

OAK PANELLING

SPECIAL STEPS WERE USED TO REACH THE HIGHEST SHELVES

A LIBRARY CHAIR WITH A BOOK REST WAS DESIGNED TO BE SAT ON BACK TO FRONT

WRITING SET WITH INKWELLS

CIGAR BOX

A GLOBE

SEALING WAX

LETTER OPENER

BOOK CARRIER

THE MOST EXPENSIVE BOOKS WERE BOUND IN LEATHER

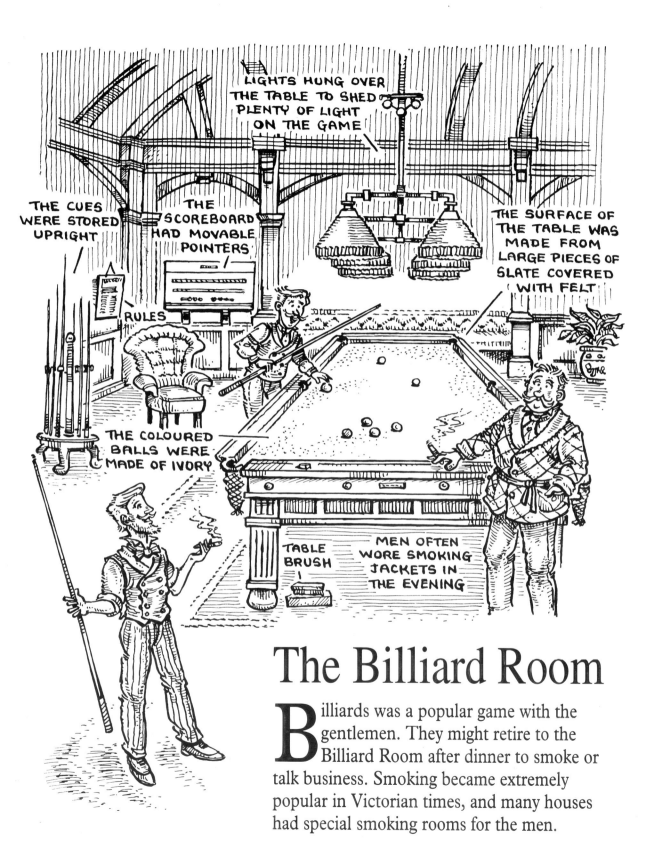

LIGHTS HUNG OVER THE TABLE TO SHED PLENTY OF LIGHT ON THE GAME

THE CUES WERE STORED UPRIGHT

THE SCOREBOARD HAD MOVABLE POINTERS

THE SURFACE OF THE TABLE WAS MADE FROM LARGE PIECES OF SLATE COVERED WITH FELT

RULES

THE COLOURED BALLS WERE MADE OF IVORY

TABLE BRUSH

MEN OFTEN WORE SMOKING JACKETS IN THE EVENING

The Billiard Room

Billiards was a popular game with the gentlemen. They might retire to the Billiard Room after dinner to smoke or talk business. Smoking became extremely popular in Victorian times, and many houses had special smoking rooms for the men.

THE NIGHT NURSERY
HAD DIFFERENT BEDS
FOR CHILDREN OF
DIFFERENT AGES

NANNY WAS
USUALLY
STRICT WITH
THE CHILDREN

PICTURES AND
A FRIEZE
BRIGHTENED
THE WALLS

STARCHED
APRON

CRADLE

COT

HALF
COT

EVERYTHING NANNY
NEEDED FOR THE BABY
COULD BE CARRIED AROUND

CHAMBER
POT

NIGHTSHIRT

STONE HOT
WATER BOTTLE

The Nurseries and Schoolroom

Victorian families were usually large – the Queen and Prince Albert, for example, had nine children. Parents were very strict and believed children should be seen and not heard. Most of their time was spent at the top of the house with a nanny, in the Day and Night Nurseries. She took them for walks, ate meals with them, bathed them and put them to bed.

The Victorians were really the first to dress their children in proper children's clothes. Little girls wore heavy dresses with knickerbockers and petticoats, while sailor suits were popular for the boys. Many of the toys in the Nursery were educational: building bricks, jigsaw puzzles and a Noah's Ark. Rocking horses were extremely popular and, of course, every nursery had a doll's house. With the invention of the railways, and later the motorcar, mechanical toy trains and cars became very popular too.

NEEDLEWORK SAMPLER

DOLLS HAD CHINA HEADS, ARMS AND LEGS

MINIATURE FURNITURE FOR THE DOLL'S HOUSE WAS HAND-MADE BY CRAFTSMEN

ROCKING HORSE

NURSERY RHYME BOOK

SCRAPBOOK

CARVED WOODEN ANIMALS BELONGED TO THE NOAH'S ARK

SOLDIERS

In the Schoolroom a governess gave lessons to the children. The most important subjects were reading, writing and arithmetic. Boys were sent away to school when they were quite young but girls stayed at home and learnt how to be young ladies.

CHILDREN WROTE THEIR LESSONS ON SLATES WITH CHALK

Bedrooms and Dressing Rooms

Victorian women took hours to get dressed and changed their clothes several times during the day. It was the fashion to wear tight corsets and bustles underneath layers of material. A lady's maid was needed to help with all the buckles, buttons and laces. She also did her mistress's hair and looked after her clothes. The master and mistress of the house had separate dressing rooms, where their clothes were stored.

HAT BOX

IN THE DRESSING ROOM, CLOTHES WERE NEATLY STORE IN WARDROBES WI MOTHBALLS AND HERB PILLOWS

WASHSTAND

BELL PULL

A POLISHED BRASS BED

A SILVER HANDMIRROR AND HAIRBRUSHES WERE KEPT ON THE DRESSING TABLE

THE DAY BED OR CHAISE LONGUE

A WRITING DESK

Every morning a jug of hot water for washing was brought up to the bedrooms by one of the maids. When everyone had got up, the maids cleaned the rooms and emptied the chamber pots.

THERE WAS A WATER TANK AT THE TOP OF THE SHOWER. WHEN THE CHAIN WAS PULLED A VALVE OPENED AND THE WATER SPRINKLED DOWN THROUGH A SIEVE ONTO THE BATHER BELOW

WASHSTAND WITH A JUG AND BOWL

A HIP BATH WAS PLACED IN FRONT OF THE FIRE TO KEEP THE WATER AND THE BATHER WARM

THE FIREPLACE HAD A SHUTTER TO PREVENT DRAUGHTS WHEN NOT IN USE

WATER CARRIER

VICTORIANS WERE ALSO KEEN ON COLD BATHS

The Bathroom

Some Victorian houses had a hand-pumped shower, but most ladies would have preferred a leisurely soak in the tub. The hot water was brought up by the maids from the Kitchen in buckets and was kept warm by the charcoal fire in the Bathroom. The maids then had to carry the dirty water back downstairs and clean out the bath.

The Dining Room

This was one of the most important rooms in a large Victorian house. Breakfast was eaten between 9 and 11 am: hot dishes, such as sausage, bacon and sometimes even game birds were served. Lunch was also informal but dinner, starting at about 7 pm, lasted for several hours and was usually a very formal meal. The table would have been highly decorated, with flower arrangements and bowls piled high with fruit. Menus were written in French, listing at least five courses: soup, a fish dish, poultry, meat and several puddings (with a different wine for each course).

THE WINE COOLER WAS FILLED WITH ICE

MEN OFTEN WORE A MONOCLE IN ONE EYE INSTEAD OF GLASSES IT WAS HUNG ROUND THEIR NECK ON A PIECE OF RIBBON

FAN

IT WAS FASHIONABLE TO FOLD NAPKINS INTO DECORATIVE SHAPES

A CHINA MENU

THE HOSTESS ARRANGED WHERE THE GUESTS SAT

AT A FORMAL DINNER PARTY, MEN WORE WHITE TIES AND BLACK SUITS, WHILE THE LADIES WORE SMART DRESSES AND LONG GLOVES

THE BUTLER SUPERVISED THE FOOTMEN, WHO SERVED FOOD TO THE GUESTS

The food was heated up on a hot plate before it was served, as it had usually gone cold by the time it got to the Dining Room. Kitchens were often a long way from Dining Rooms in Victorian times so that people eating their meals were not put off by strong cooking smells.

CANDLES IN ELABORATE CANDLESTICKS PROVIDED SUBTLE LIGHTING FOR MEALS

BUTLER

THE SIDEBOARD HELD ALL THAT THE SERVANTS NEEDED TO SERVE AT TABLE

SILVER VEGETABLE DISHES

KNIFE BOX

CUT GLASS WINE GLASSES AND FINGER BOWLS

HOT PLATE

BRUSH AND PAN TO CLEAN UP CRUMBS

LADIES WORE THEIR HAIR PILED UP ON TOP OF THEIR HEADS ON FORMAL OCCASIONS

WATER URN

IF THE DINING ROOM WAS UPSTAIRS, THE FOOD WAS OFTEN BROUGHT UP FROM THE KITCHEN IN A 'DUMB WAITER'- A SMALL LIFT

The Kitchen

This huge room was bustling with activity from dawn to dusk. The maids were up at 6 am, cleaning and polishing copper pots and pans. It took the cook and her team many hours to prepare all the meals.

LARGE HIGH WINDOWS FOR LIGHT AND VENTILATION

CANDLE BOX

THE KITCHEN RANGE HAD A HOTPLATE ON TOP FOR KEEPING THE POTS WARM

WASTE

STOCKPO

BAIN-MARIE

⑧

SUGAR WAS BOUGHT IN LARGE LOAVES THEN CUT INTO SMALLER LUMPS

A PESTLE AND MORTAR WAS USED FOR CRUSHING INGREDIENTS

THE INSIDE OF THE OVEN WAS USED FOR ROASTING OR BAKING

B

⑦

⑥

FOOD HAD TO BE PROTECTED FROM MICE

⑤

PC M

ICE CREAM FREEZER

FOOD WAS PREPARED ON WELL SCRUBBED WOODEN TABLES

④

When a large dinner party was being prepared, the Kitchen would have been a hot and smelly place, with vegetables boiling on the range, poultry turning on a spit, meat roasting in the oven and puddings and pies steaming in their dishes.

THE HIGH CEILING TOOK AWAY SOME OF THE SMOKE AND STEAM

COOK MADE SURE THE COPPER SAUCEPANS WERE POLISHED UNTIL THEY SHONE

I ~ WANT NOT

KETTLE ON THE HOB

WATER CISTERN

DUMB WAITER THE OTHER END OF THE LIFT

①

JELLY MOULD

SPIT

THE DRIPPING TRAY UNDERNEATH THE SPIT WAS TO CATCH FAT AND JUICES

A DUTCH OVEN OR 'HASTENER' REFLECTED HEAT FROM THE OPEN FIRE ON TO THE MEAT

②

EAL HER

ALL SORTS OF KNIVES AND CHOPPERS WERE USED

③

ME WORK SURFACES SLID NAY WHEN NOT IN USE

Many strange-looking tools and gadgets would have been used in a Victorian kitchen. Can you guess the uses of the numbered objects in this picture? Answers on the final page.

The Scullery, Dry Store, Larders and Still Room

As well as the Kitchen, there were other rooms used for preparing and storing food. Vegetables were cleaned and chopped in the Scullery, where there was a supply of running water. After a meal the maids did the washing-up here in great wooden sinks and then left the plates to drain in the plate racks.

THERE WAS SPACE FOR HUNDREDS OF PLATES TO DRY ON THE PLATE-RACK

SCULLERYMAIDS WERE USUALLY VERY YOUNG GIRLS OF EIGHT OR NINE

THE CHINA PLATES AND CUPS WERE STORED IN A LARGE DRESSER

FISH AND VEGETABLES WERE CLEANED AT THE SINK

WOODEN SINKS WERE LINED WITH SLATE

PLATE PAIL

MAIDS WORE THEIR HAIR TIED BACK AND A PINAFORE FOR CLEANLINESS

DUCKBOARD TO KEEP YOUR FEET DRY

SUGAR WAS KEPT ON THE TOP SHELF SO THAT MICE COULD NOT REACH IT

PEPPER MILL

DRIED HERBS WERE HUNG IN MUSLIN BAGS

SPICES

TEA

THE SOAP WAS KEPT IN A SEPARATE CUPBOARD

The Dry Store was for ingredients such as tea, coffee, sugar, spices, dried fruit and rice. They were kept in drawers and tins which could hold several months' supply. Candles were also kept here.

Large houses had several larders for storing food. Salted meat, such as ham and bacon, hung from the ceiling in the meat larder. Cheeses, eggs, fruit, vegetables, bread and other things you would now keep in a refrigerator were stored in another larder on slate shelves to keep them cool. Some houses also had a fish larder.

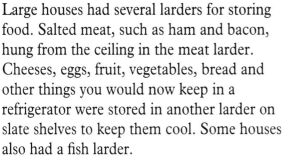

A MEAT SAFE

THE WINDOWS WERE COVERED WITH MESH RATHER THAN GLASS TO KEEP THE ROOM AS COOL AS POSSIBLE

WHITE WALLS

MEAT CAME FROM THE HOME FARM. IT WAS SALTED BEFORE BEING HUNG FROM IRON HOOKS

WOODEN CHOPPING BLOCK

MUSLIN WAS USED TO COVER THE FRUIT AND VEGETABLES

A BRICK FLOOR WITH A DRAIN FOR EASY CLEANING

SLOP PAIL

STRING MOP

A PAIR OF BRASS SCALES AND WEIGHTS WERE USED FOR MEASURING INGREDIENTS

BRICK LINED BAKING OVEN

A TEA KETTLE

PASTRY CUTTERS AND A ROLLING PIN

THE TEA SERVICE WAS USED BY THE MAIDS

The Still Room was used for making jams and other preserves. There was also a small oven in here for baking. Tea was often prepared in the Still Room so that nobody got in the way when dinner was being cooked in the Kitchen.

The Housekeeper's Room and the Butler's Pantry

The housekeeper was in charge of all the female servants and organised their duties. She discussed the daily menu with the mistress of the house every morning, then gave instructions to the cook. She would sometimes ask the butler to take tea in her Sitting Room.

THE HOUSEKEEPER'S ROOM WAS COSY AND WARM WITH A SMALL FIREPLACE AND COMFORTABLE ARMCHAIRS

THE KEYS IN HER BASKET SHOWED THAT SHE WAS IN CHARGE

PORTRAIT OF QUEEN VICTORIA

WINDSOR CHAIR

SEWING MACHINE

WORKBOX

OIL LAMP

ONE OF THE HOUSEKEEPER'S JOBS WAS TO MEND THE LINEN. THE SEWING MACHINE WAS WORKED BY TURNING A HANDLE TO MOVE THE NEEDLE UP AND DOWN

BELLS TO CALL THE SERVANTS RANG IN THE CORRIDOR OUTSIDE. EACH BELL RANG A DIFFERENT NOTE TO SIGNAL WHERE SERVICE WAS NEEDED

The butler also had his own room, where he kept some of the silver and linen. He decanted the wine for lunch, supper and dinner in his Pantry and changed into his smart evening clothes here. The butler was also responsible for other storage rooms like the Cellar, the Gun Room, the Lamp Room and the Brushing Room.

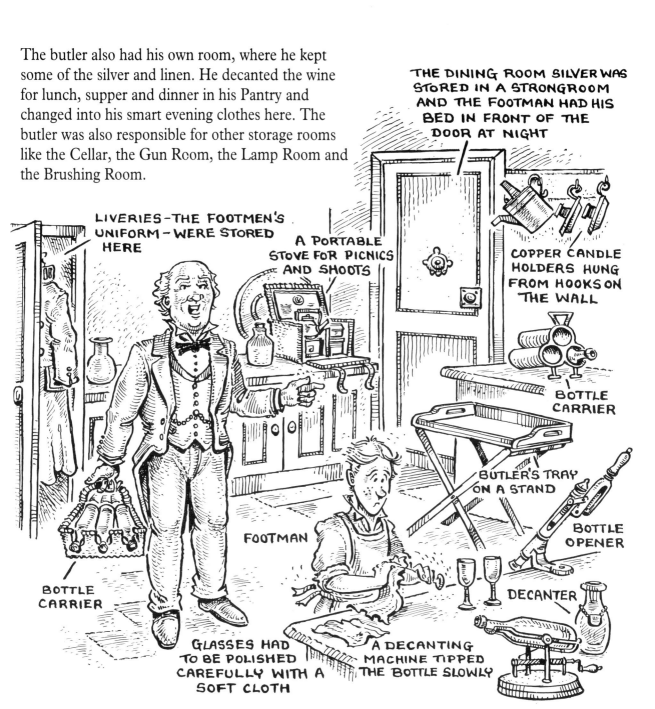

THE DINING ROOM SILVER WAS STORED IN A STRONGROOM AND THE FOOTMAN HAD HIS BED IN FRONT OF THE DOOR AT NIGHT

LIVERIES - THE FOOTMEN'S UNIFORM - WERE STORED HERE

A PORTABLE STOVE FOR PICNICS AND SHOOTS

COPPER CANDLE HOLDERS HUNG FROM HOOKS ON THE WALL

BOTTLE CARRIER

BUTLER'S TRAY ON A STAND

BOTTLE OPENER

FOOTMAN

DECANTER

BOTTLE CARRIER

GLASSES HAD TO BE POLISHED CAREFULLY WITH A SOFT CLOTH

A DECANTING MACHINE TIPPED THE BOTTLE SLOWLY

All the servants ate their meals together in the Servants' Hall. This would have been a large room with one long table in the centre. Everyone sat in strict order of importance, with the butler at the head of the table. Grace was said before anyone could start to eat. Table manners were just as important 'downstairs'.

The Dairy

THE STONE SURFACES AND ALL THE EQUIPMENT IN THE DAIRY WERE KEPT VERY CLEAN

Milk was delivered to the Dairy every morning from the home farm. The dairymaids would have shivered in this cold room while they churned the cream to make butter. The Dairy had to be cool at all times to keep the milk fresh. Cheese-making was a long and difficult job, while butter making was quicker, but turning the handle of the butter churn was hard work.

WHEN THE MILK ARRIVED IT WAS POURED INTO PANS STANDING IN COLD WATER IN A TROUGH

PANS OF MILK WERE HEATED ON A SCALDING-RANGE TO MAKE CLOTTED CREAM

A PLUNGER CHURN

NEXT THE CREAM WAS MIXED IN A WOODEN CHURN TO MAKE BUTTER

THE END-OVER-END CHURN WAS TURNED OVER AND OVER

BUTTER MAKING

A CREAM SKIMMER

FIRST THE MILK HAD TO BE SEPARATED FROM THE CREAM. THIS WAS DONE BY LEAVING MILK IN A WIDE PAN FOR TWENTY-FOUR HOURS AND THEN SKIMMING OFF THE CREAM

Iced puddings and blancmanges, very popular with the Victorians, were prepared in the Dairy, and stored on a marble slab. Jellies and custards were also made here for the Nursery.

O MAKE CHEESE
IE MILK WAS
RDLED, THE CURDS
RE SEPARATED
OM THE LIQUID
ID FINALLY PUT
A CHEESE PRESS

PATTERNED TILES DECORATED THE WALLS OF THE DAIRY. THEY WERE ALSO EASY TO KEEP CLEAN

SOME DAIRIES HAD SPRING WATER CHANNELLED ALONG THE SHELVES TO COOL THEM FOR STORAGE

CHEESE PRESS

FINALLY, WHEN THE BUTTER WAS DRY IT WAS PATTED INTO SHAPE WITH A PAIR OF WOODEN BOARDS CALLED SCOTCH BOARDS

THE BUTTER THEN WENT THROUGH A BUTTERWORKER

BUTTER SCALES

BUTTER BOARD

THE WATER WAS SQUEEZED OUT BY A MOVING ROLLER

BUTTER PATS PRINTED PRETTY SHAPES AND PATTERNS ON THE BUTTER

The Laundry

Washing and caring for the household's clothes, table and bed linen was a full-time job for at least three laundrymaids. The Laundry was usually in a separate building with several rooms for washing and drying. Clothes were washed in different-sized tubs and barrels, and scrubbed against a washboard. A mangle was used to squeeze out the water, then the clothes were hung on racks or in closets to dry (on windy days they were hung outside).

THE PEG DOLLY WAS TWISTED ROUND AND ROUND – IT HELPED TO WASH THE CLOTHES

THE WET LAUNDRY

WATER PUMP

LINEN WAS BLEACHED OUTSIDE TO MAKE IT WHITE

CLOTHES WERE RUBBED CLEAN AGAINST A WASHBOARD

THE 'COPPER' WITH A COAL FIRE UNDERNEATH BOILED THE WATER

SPILLED WATER WAS DRAINED OFF

PATTENS RAISED THE MAIDS' FEET ABOVE A WET FLOOR

THE MANGLE SQUEEZED THE EXCESS WATER OUT BETWEEN TWO ROLLERS

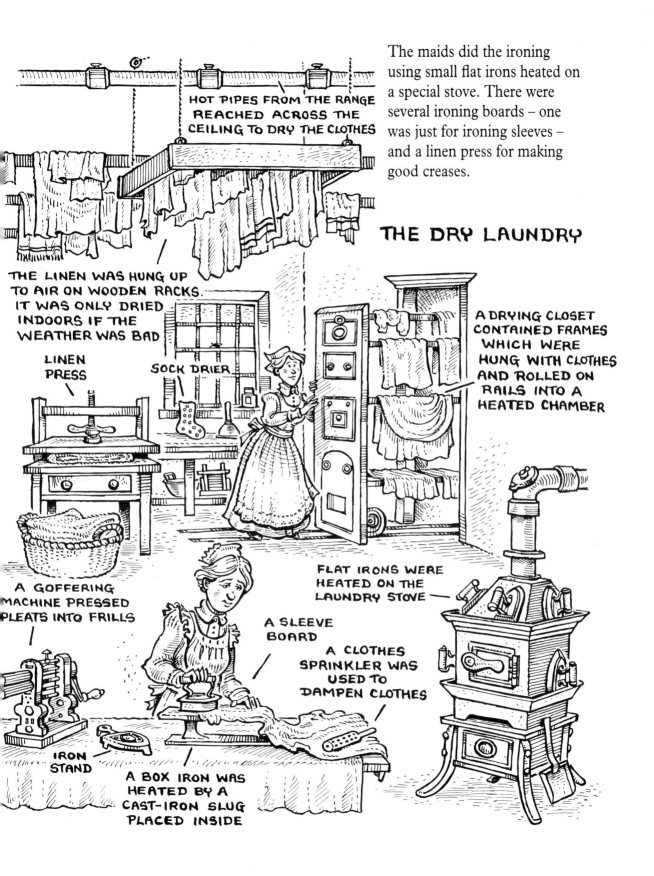

HOT PIPES FROM THE RANGE REACHED ACROSS THE CEILING TO DRY THE CLOTHES

The maids did the ironing using small flat irons heated on a special stove. There were several ironing boards – one was just for ironing sleeves – and a linen press for making good creases.

THE LINEN WAS HUNG UP TO AIR ON WOODEN RACKS. IT WAS ONLY DRIED INDOORS IF THE WEATHER WAS BAD

THE DRY LAUNDRY

LINEN PRESS

SOCK DRIER

A DRYING CLOSET CONTAINED FRAMES WHICH WERE HUNG WITH CLOTHES AND ROLLED ON RAILS INTO A HEATED CHAMBER

A GOFFERING MACHINE PRESSED PLEATS INTO FRILLS

A SLEEVE BOARD

FLAT IRONS WERE HEATED ON THE LAUNDRY STOVE

A CLOTHES SPRINKLER WAS USED TO DAMPEN CLOTHES

IRON STAND

A BOX IRON WAS HEATED BY A CAST-IRON SLUG PLACED INSIDE

The Conservatory

Some of the grander Victorian houses had conservatories. Large sheets of glass could now be produced, and these were used to create impressive new buildings, like the famous 'Crystal Palace', built specially for the Great Exhibition in 1851. Conservatories usually were joined to the house, connecting with the Drawing Room or the Library, to provide a peaceful place to sit and talk amongst all the greenery.

PALM

THE CONSERVATORY HAD TO BE KEPT WARM FOR THE EXOTIC PLANTS TO GROW — USING HEATED WATER PIPES

YUCCA

BAMBOO

THERE WERE PATHS FOR WANDERING ROMANTICALLY AMONG THE PLANTS

THERMOMETER

IN THE HOT ATMOSPHERE THE PLANTS NEEDED CAREFUL ATTENTION AND WATERING

REVOLVING FLOWER POTS WERE TURNED A QUARTER-TURN EACH DAY TO PROVIDE AN EVEN AMOUNT OF SUNLIGHT

GERANIUM PLANTS FLOWER DURING THE WINTER

TO KEEP THE CONSERVATORY AT ITS BEST, PLANTS WERE CHANGED AND REPOTTED REGULARLY

THE GLASS SHEETS WERE FASTENED ONTO A CAST-IRON FRAME WHICH COULD COVER A LARGE AREA

TINKLING FOUNTAINS ADDED TO THE PLEASANT ATMOSPHERE

ORANGE TREES

THIS WAS A SWEET-SMELLING PLACE TO ENJOY AFTERNOON TEA

THE FURNITURE HERE WAS DIFFERENT FROM THAT IN THE HOUSE. IT WAS OFTEN MADE OF CANE

FLOWERS FROM THE CONSERVATORY WERE USED TO DECORATE THE HOUSE DURING THE WINTER

AMONG THE PLANTS WERE STATUES AND CLASSICAL URNS

The Victorians liked to collect exotic plants from different countries. Palms, ferns, bamboo trees and orchids flourished in the Conservatory, and orange and lemon trees were kept in here during the winter, then taken outside into the garden when the weather was warmer.

The Kitchen Garden

The Kitchen Garden was surrounded by a wall to protect plants from bad weather and rabbits. This also meant it was out of the view from the main rooms of the house. Neat rows of vegetables and fruit were grown to provide food for the household, and cut flowers for decorations. Manure from the stables would be used as fertilizer.

ORCHARD

THE GREENHOUSE MADE IT POSSIBLE TO GROW VEGETABLES OUT OF SEASON

FRUIT TREES WERE FAN-TRAINED ON SOUTH-FACING WALLS

BEEHIVES

ROWS OF SPINAC CAULIFLOWERS, CARROTS AND RUN BEANS WERE GRO

A YOUNG GARDEN BOY COLLECTED THE VEGETABLES COOK NEEDED EACH MORNING

BIRD SCARER

CLAY FORCING POTS WERE USED TO MAKE RHUBARE GROW TALL

YOUNG LETTUCES WERE GROWN UNDER GLASS TO PROTECT THEM FROM THE FROST

COOK USED A WIDE VARIETY OF HERBS

A CLOCHE

LANTERN CLOCHE

CARDOON WAS A VICTORIAN WINTER VEGETABLE. IT WAS LIKE A GIANT CELERY

THE USEFUL WHEELBARROW

THE HEAD GARDENER ORGANISED ALL THE GARDENERS AND APPRENTICES

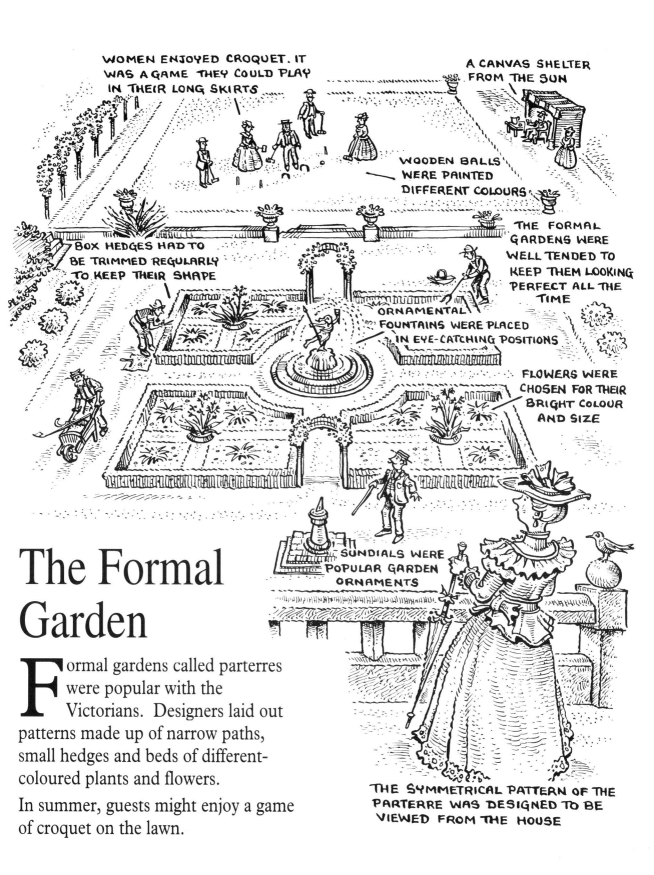

WOMEN ENJOYED CROQUET. IT WAS A GAME THEY COULD PLAY IN THEIR LONG SKIRTS

A CANVAS SHELTER FROM THE SUN

WOODEN BALLS WERE PAINTED DIFFERENT COLOURS

BOX HEDGES HAD TO BE TRIMMED REGULARLY TO KEEP THEIR SHAPE

THE FORMAL GARDENS WERE WELL TENDED TO KEEP THEM LOOKING PERFECT ALL THE TIME

ORNAMENTAL FOUNTAINS WERE PLACED IN EYE-CATCHING POSITIONS

FLOWERS WERE CHOSEN FOR THEIR BRIGHT COLOUR AND SIZE

SUNDIALS WERE POPULAR GARDEN ORNAMENTS

The Formal Garden

Formal gardens called parterres were popular with the Victorians. Designers laid out patterns made up of narrow paths, small hedges and beds of different-coloured plants and flowers.

In summer, guests might enjoy a game of croquet on the lawn.

THE SYMMETRICAL PATTERN OF THE PARTERRE WAS DESIGNED TO BE VIEWED FROM THE HOUSE

The Home Farm

There were many different jobs on the home farm. A stockman looked after the cows that supplied the milk for the Dairy. There was also a pigman, a shepherd, a blacksmith and agricultural workers to plough the fields and bring in the harvest.

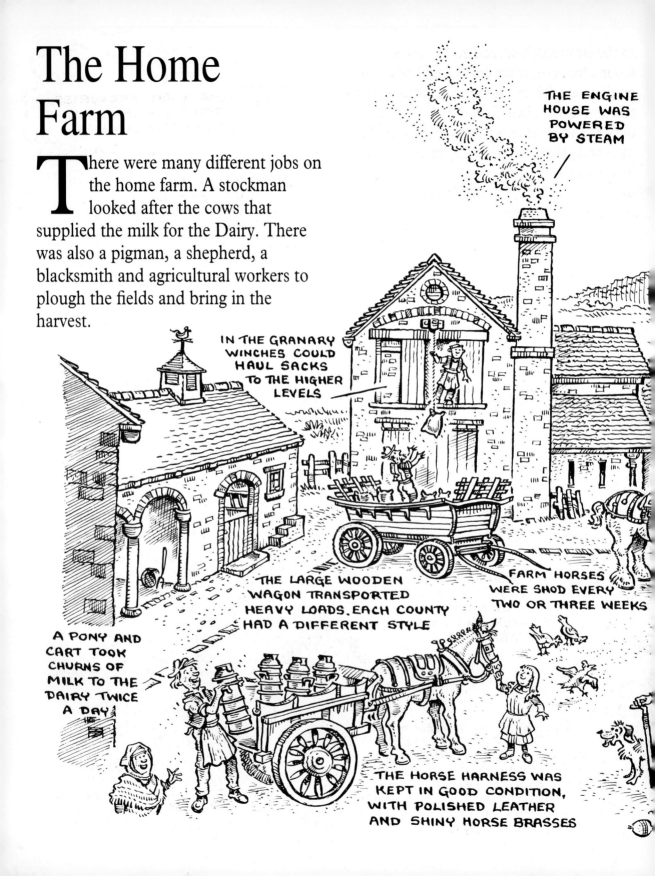

THE ENGINE HOUSE WAS POWERED BY STEAM

IN THE GRANARY WINCHES COULD HAUL SACKS TO THE HIGHER LEVELS

THE LARGE WOODEN WAGON TRANSPORTED HEAVY LOADS. EACH COUNTY HAD A DIFFERENT STYLE

FARM HORSES WERE SHOD EVERY TWO OR THREE WEEKS

A PONY AND CART TOOK CHURNS OF MILK TO THE DAIRY TWICE A DAY

THE HORSE HARNESS WAS KEPT IN GOOD CONDITION, WITH POLISHED LEATHER AND SHINY HORSE BRASSES

In the farmyard, hens and geese pecked around for corn, while ducks could be found on the pond. Their eggs were gathered up and taken to the Kitchen. Pigs were kept in the piggery and enormous shire horses for pulling carts and ploughs lived in the stables. Grain was stored in the granary where noisy machines crushed and pounded barley and oats into animal feed.

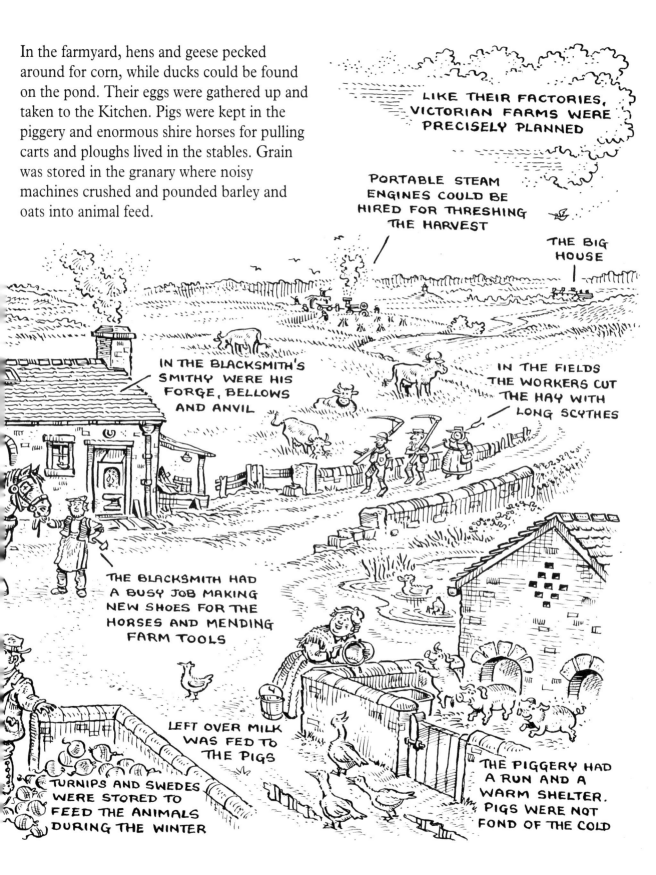

LIKE THEIR FACTORIES, VICTORIAN FARMS WERE PRECISELY PLANNED

PORTABLE STEAM ENGINES COULD BE HIRED FOR THRESHING THE HARVEST

THE BIG HOUSE

IN THE BLACKSMITH'S SMITHY WERE HIS FORGE, BELLOWS AND ANVIL

IN THE FIELDS THE WORKERS CUT THE HAY WITH LONG SCYTHES

THE BLACKSMITH HAD A BUSY JOB MAKING NEW SHOES FOR THE HORSES AND MENDING FARM TOOLS

LEFT OVER MILK WAS FED TO THE PIGS

TURNIPS AND SWEDES WERE STORED TO FEED THE ANIMALS DURING THE WINTER

THE PIGGERY HAD A RUN AND A WARM SHELTER. PIGS WERE NOT FOND OF THE COLD

Victorian National Trust Houses

The Argory, Northern Ireland
Carlyle's House, London
Cragside, Northumbria
Knightshayes Court, Devon
Lanhydrock, Cornwall
Penrhyn Castle, Gwynedd
Standen, West Sussex
Wightwick Manor, West Midlands

Other National Trust Houses with Interesting Servants' Quarters

Ardress, Northern Ireland
Beningbrough Hall, North Yorkshire
Calke Abbey, Derbyshire
Castle Drogo, Devon
Castle Ward, County Down
Dunham Massey, Cheshire
Erddig, North Wales
Kingston Lacy, Dorset
Lyme Park, Cheshire
Osterley Park, London
Shugborough, Staffordshire
Speke Hall, Merseyside
Tatton Park, Cheshire
Wimpole Hall and Home Farm,
Cambridgeshire

First published 1993 by National Trust Enterprises Ltd,
36 Queen Anne's Gate, London SW1H 9AS
Registered Charity No. 205846
© The National Trust 1993
Reprinted 1994
ISBN 0 7078 0169 9
Edited by Jo Fletcher-Watson
Designed by Roger Warham, Blade Communications
Production by Bob Towell
Printed by Grafedit S.p.A., Italy

ANSWERS to Kitchen Quiz

1. Coffee percolator

2. Knife cleaner

3. Egg cutter

4. Spinach press

5. Raisin stoner

6. Sugar nippers

7. Sausage maker

8. Wall salt for storing salt